Leaping Lizards!

TEACHING ALLITERATION

BY LISA OWINGS

The Child's World®
childsworld.com

Published by The Child's World®
1980 Lookout Drive • Mankato, MN 56003-1705
800-599-READ • www.childsworld.com

ACKNOWLEDGMENTS
The Child's World®: Mary Swensen, Publishing Director
Red Line Editorial: Editorial direction and production
The Design Lab: Design

Photographs ©: iStockphoto, cover (top), 1, 5; Hein Welman/
Shutterstock Images, cover (bottom), 2-3; Tim Booth/Shutterstock
Images, 6; Nejron Photo/Shutterstock Images, 8; Ian Duffield/
Shutterstock Images, 8-9; Shutterstock Images, 10-11, 14;
Anan Kaewkhammul/Shutterstock Images, 12; Michal Ninger/
Shutterstock Images, 13

ISBN 9781503808386
LCCN 2015958421

Printed in the United States of America
Mankato, MN
June, 2016
PA02304

ABOUT THE AUTHOR
Lisa Owings has a degree in English and
creative writing from the University of
Minnesota. She has written and edited a wide
variety of educational books for young people.
Lisa lives in Andover, Minnesota.

Alliteration means using words that **s**tart with the **s**ame **s**ound. **S**ee? Look for **alliteration** in this book. You will find repeating sounds in **bold** type.

Leroy is a **l**izard. He **r**ests on a **r**ough **r**ock.
A **s**lithering **s**nake **s**tartles him.
He takes a **l**ong **l**eap into the air!

Sam the **s**nake is **s**neaky. He **s**lithers and **s**lides **s**ilently past.

Pete the **p**arrot **f**lies **f**ar. His **w**ings **wh**isper on the **w**ind. He **f**lies with his **f**lock of **f**riends.

Jake the **j**aguar **r**oars and **r**oams.
His **c**olorful **c**oat **h**elps **h**im **h**ide while **h**e **h**unts.

Myrtle the **m**onkey **sp**ies Jake's **sp**ots. **Sh**e **sh**rieks and **h**eads **h**ome in a **h**urry.

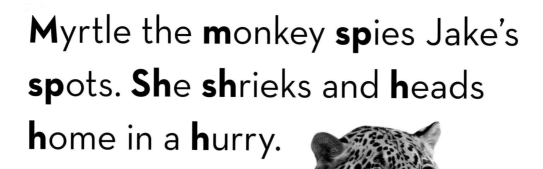

The **f**orest is **f**ull of animal **f**riends who **r**un and **r**omp. When the **s**un **s**ets, they **s**ay, "**S**o long!"

Did you hear alliteration?

coat, colorful
far, flies,
   flock,
   forest,
   friends, full
heads, helps,
   hide, him,
   home,
   hunts, hurry
jaguar, Jake
leap, Leroy,
   lizard, long
monkey,
   Myrtle
parrot, Pete

rests, roams,
   roars,
   rock, romp,
   rough, run
Sam, say,
   sets,
   silently,
   slides,
   slithering,
   slithers,
   snake,
   sneaky, so,
   startles, sun
she, shrieks
spies, spots
whisper,
   wind, wings

To Learn More

IN THE LIBRARY
Archer, Felix. *A Little Book of Alliterations*. Great Britain: Inside, 2010.

Hills, Tad. *R Is for Rocket: An ABC Book*. New York: Schwartz & Wade, 2015.

Lewis, Patrick J., ed. *National Geographic Book of Animal Poetry: 200 Poems that Squeak, Soar, and Roar*. Washington, DC: National Geographic, 2012.

ON THE WEB
Visit our Web site for links about alliteration: **childsworld.com/links**

Note to Parents, Teachers, and Librarians: We routinely verify our Web links to make sure they are safe and active sites. So encourage your readers to check them out!